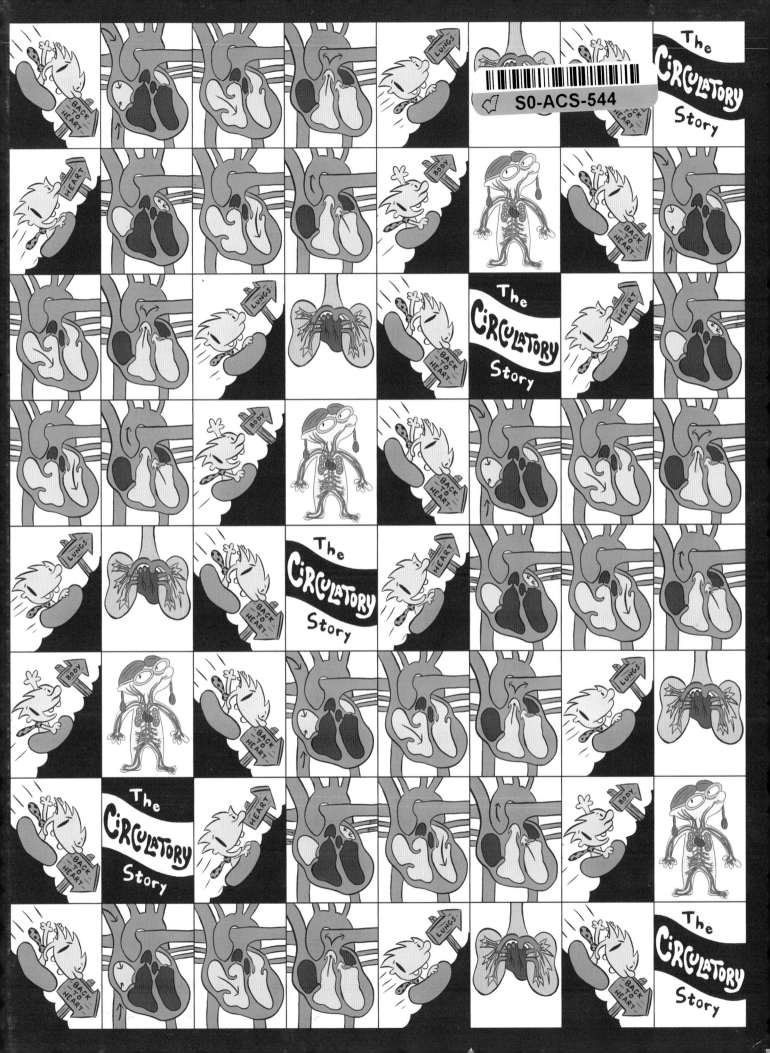

THE CIRCULATORY STORY

Mary K. Corcoran

Illustrated by Jef Czekaj

Charlesbridge

For Eileen, Forrest, and Matthew, who live in
my heart—M. K. C.

For my mother, Lorraine Christensen—J. C.

Published by Charlesbridge
85 Main Street
Watertown, MA 02472
(617) 926-0329
www.charlesbridge.com

Library of Congress Cataloging-in-Publication Data
Corcoran, Mary K.
    The circulatory story / Mary K. Corcoran ; illustrated by Jef Czekaj.
       p. cm.
    ISBN 978-1-58089-208-7 (reinforced for library use)
    ISBN 978-1-58089-209-4 (softcover)
1. Blood—Circulation—Juvenile literature. 2. Cardiovascular
system—Physiology—Juvenile literature. I. Czekaj, Jef, ill. II. Title.
QP103.C67 2010
612.1'3—dc22   2008025332

Printed in Singapore
(hc) 10 9 8 7 6 5 4 3 2 1
(sc) 10 9 8 7 6 5 4 3 2 1

Line art drawn in ink on Bristol and then scanned and colored
   on a MacBook Pro using Adobe Photoshop
Display type and text type set in Ogre and Cheltenham
Color separations by Chroma Graphics, Singapore
Printed and bound September 2009 by Imago in Singapore
Production supervision by Brian G. Walker
Designed by Martha MacLeod Sikkema

It's time to find out how your heart, blood, and blood vessels work together as you take the best ride of your life. It's a trip through the body's circulatory system. Your adventure begins in a tiny drop of blood.

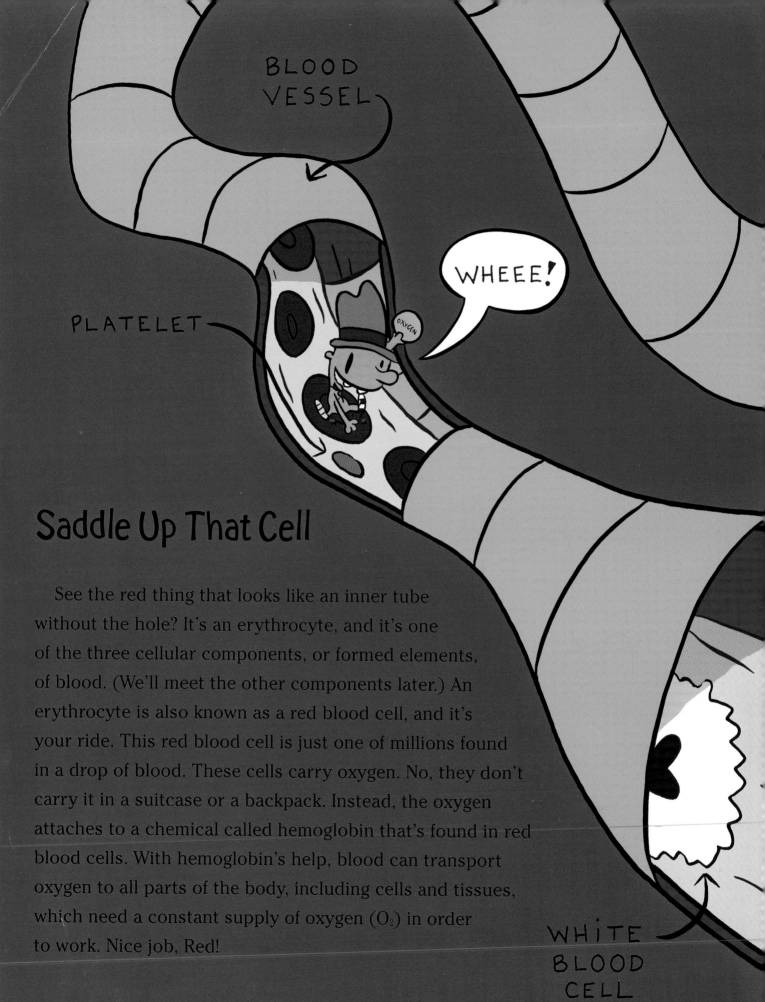

BLOOD VESSEL

PLATELET

WHEEE!

OXYGEN

WHITE BLOOD CELL

Saddle Up That Cell

See the red thing that looks like an inner tube without the hole? It's an erythrocyte, and it's one of the three cellular components, or formed elements, of blood. (We'll meet the other components later.) An erythrocyte is also known as a red blood cell, and it's your ride. This red blood cell is just one of millions found in a drop of blood. These cells carry oxygen. No, they don't carry it in a suitcase or a backpack. Instead, the oxygen attaches to a chemical called hemoglobin that's found in red blood cells. With hemoglobin's help, blood can transport oxygen to all parts of the body, including cells and tissues, which need a constant supply of oxygen (O_2) in order to work. Nice job, Red!

Go with the Flow

Busy red blood cells are always on the move. But how do they flow from one part of the body to another? The blood they travel in is full of a substance called plasma. Plasma contains some dissolved proteins, but is mostly water—about ninety percent—which lets blood flow pretty well. Without plasma, these cells would cause a traffic jam!

Your Heart, Open 24/7

Traveling on your red blood cell, the first place you'll visit is the heart. Your hardworking heart is about the size of your fist. It's located in the chest, a little toward your left side. It's enclosed in a special protective sac called the pericardium. The heart is strong and muscular and works day and night. In fact, it started beating eight months before you were born. By the time you're seventy years old, it will have beaten about 2.5 billion times.

Stay on Your Own Side

You'll notice that the heart has two sides—the right side and the left side. A thick wall called the septum separates the two sides. Each side has its own job to do. The left side receives blood from the lungs and pumps it to the whole body, while the right side receives blood from the body and pumps it to the lungs. You might think of the heart as a divided highway. A divider separates the lanes, and cars must stay in their own lane. If not, there's trouble!

MY LEFT iS YOUR RIGHT!

LEFT HAND

TO BODY

TO LUNGS

FROM BODY

FROM LUNGS

FROM LUNGS

FROM BODY

TO BODY

SEPTUM

NEXT EXIT: THE BODY

ONE WAY

ONE WAY

ZOOM

ZOOM

ZOOM

Rooms with a View

The heart not only has two sides, it also has an upstairs and a downstairs. Each side has an upstairs room and a downstairs room, and each side's upstairs and downstairs are connected. The upstairs rooms are called atria (atrium, in the singular), and the downstairs rooms are called ventricles. So in total, your heart has four rooms called chambers. Unlike the rooms in your home, these rooms have no furniture—they're empty, leaving plenty of room for blood to flow through on a consistent basis.

I WISH MY ROOM LOOKED THAT CLEAN.

LEFT ATRIUM

RIGHT ATRIUM

MITRAL VALVE

AORTIC VALVE

LEFT VENTRICLE

RIGHT VENTRICLE

TRICUSPID VALVE

PULMONARY VALVE

Beat It!

It's like Grand Central Station here in the heart, with blood flowing in and flowing out with each beat. Each time the heart beats, it squeezes and then relaxes. This action sends blood through the heart and into blood vessels that go to different parts of the body.

This left atrium is a nice place to visit, but don't get too comfortable here. You're moving down to the left ventricle. Hold on to your cell! You're going to the left ventricle the hard way—through a hole in the floor!

ATRIA SQUEEZE

VENTRICLES SQUEEZE

HOLEY-MOLEY!

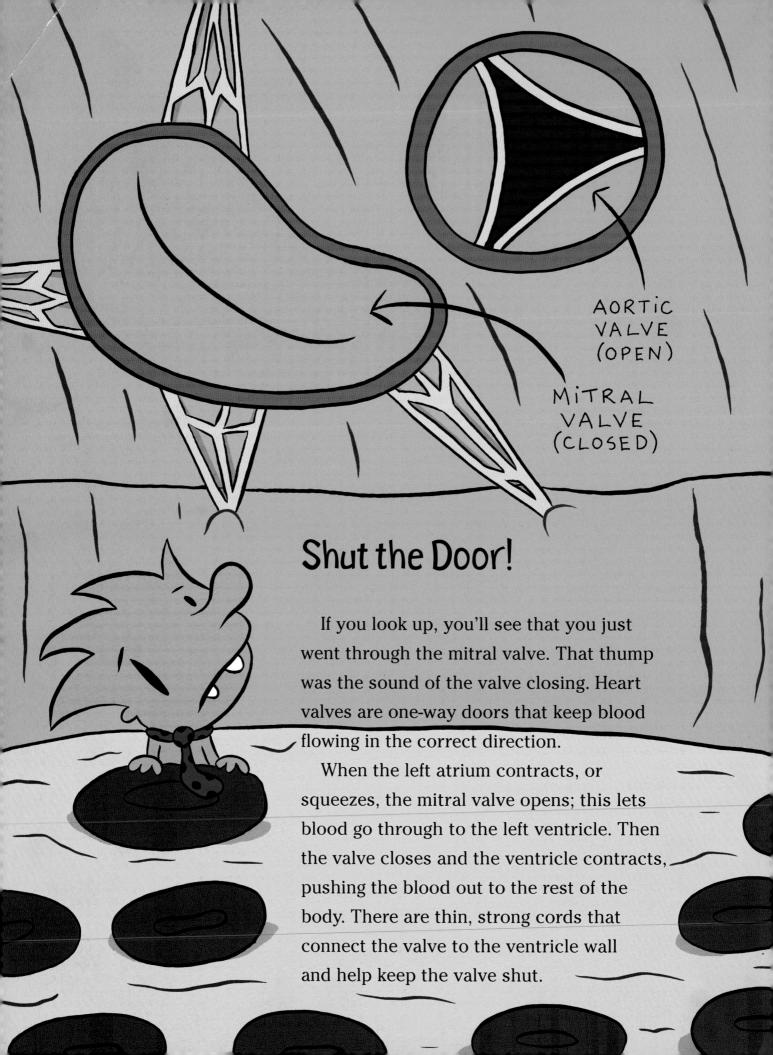

AORTIC
VALVE
(OPEN)

MITRAL
VALVE
(CLOSED)

Shut the Door!

If you look up, you'll see that you just went through the mitral valve. That thump was the sound of the valve closing. Heart valves are one-way doors that keep blood flowing in the correct direction.

When the left atrium contracts, or squeezes, the mitral valve opens; this lets blood go through to the left ventricle. Then the valve closes and the ventricle contracts, pushing the blood out to the rest of the body. There are thin, strong cords that connect the valve to the ventricle wall and help keep the valve shut.

Like most pumps, the heart can function with slightly leaky valves. With more serious valve problems, the valve doesn't close or stay closed properly; this lets blood flow back from the ventricle into the atrium. This makes the heart have to work harder, which could damage it. But when everything works well, blood goes through the valve and keeps going where it is supposed to go.

Pumped Up

The left ventricle is a mega-muscular chamber. Its walls are thick and strong. They have to be, because they pump blood out of the heart and send it to the rest of the body. That's where you're headed, too.

Around the World

Blood doesn't just slosh around in your body after it leaves the heart. First it goes through another valve, the aortic valve. Then it travels through blood vessels, which are like the tunnels of a super subway system. The main goal of blood vessels is to nourish body cells by bringing them things that they need, like oxygen. Blood travels throughout the entire body in different types of blood vessels. The main kinds of blood vessels are arteries, capillaries, and veins. Arteries carry blood away from the heart. Veins carry blood to the heart. Capillaries connect arteries and veins.

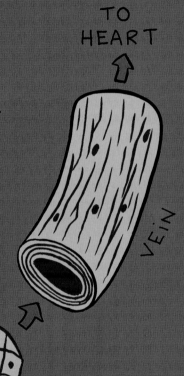

BLOOD TO HEART

VEIN

CAPILLARY

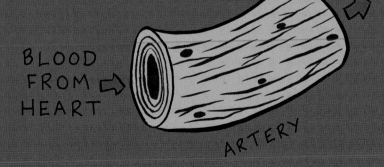

BLOOD FROM HEART

ARTERY

If all the blood vessels in the human body were lined up end to end, you'd have to travel about sixty thousand miles to get from one end to the other. That's equivalent to going around the world twice!

The Arching Aorta

Arteries are big. All arteries have thick, elastic walls. These walls have three layers, each with lots of give so they can expand as blood passes through them. The artery you're traveling in as you leave the left ventricle is called the aorta. It's the biggest artery in the whole body. It's an important one, too, because all blood travels through it before heading off to other places in the body.

TO HEAD, NECK, AND ARM

AORTA

PULMONARY ARTERY

FROM LEFT VENTRICLE

THE HEART

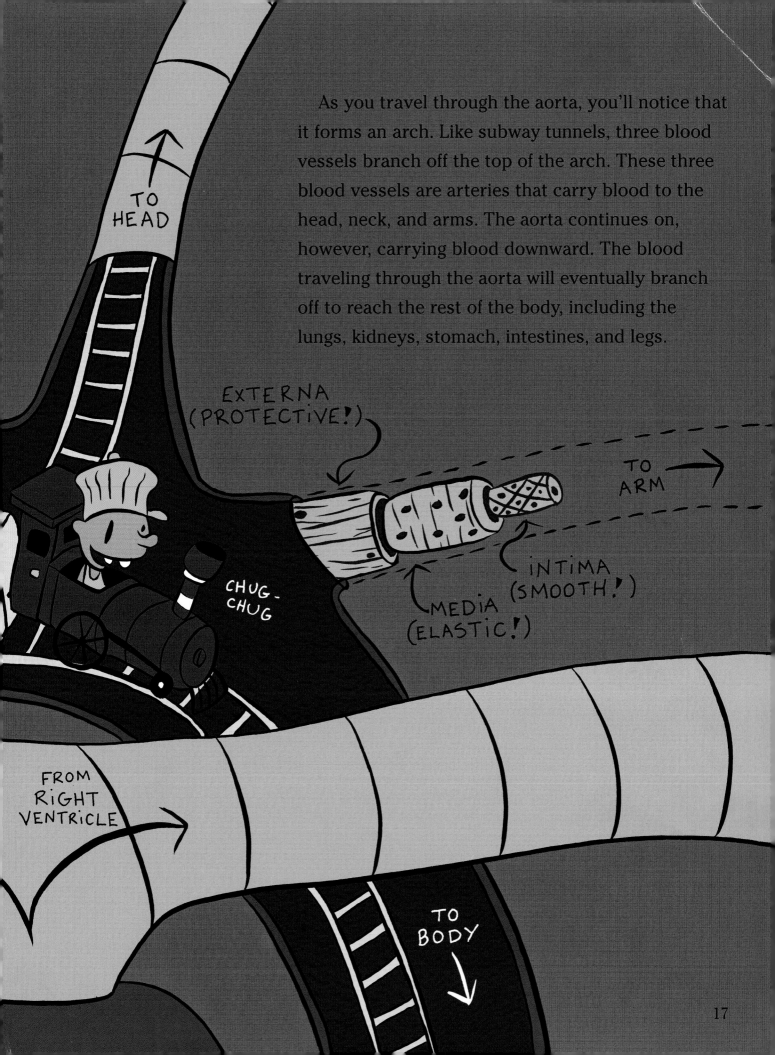

As you travel through the aorta, you'll notice that it forms an arch. Like subway tunnels, three blood vessels branch off the top of the arch. These three blood vessels are arteries that carry blood to the head, neck, and arms. The aorta continues on, however, carrying blood downward. The blood traveling through the aorta will eventually branch off to reach the rest of the body, including the lungs, kidneys, stomach, intestines, and legs.

Don't Pressure Me

Due to the pumping of the heart, blood moves through the aorta under a lot of pressure. The measurement of pressure on the walls of arteries is called blood pressure. This pressure moves blood to the smaller blood vessels. There's one now . . . it's a capillary.

This is going to be a tight squeeze!

THERE'S A LOT OF TRAFFIC TODAY.

Tiny but Terrific

Capillaries are so narrow that red blood cells pass through them one at a time. Some capillaries have more space than others, depending on where they are in the body. For example, capillaries in parts of the intestine and in the brain are narrower, or smaller in diameter, than those in the skin. Capillary walls are only one thin cell layer thick. But that's a good thing, because . . . whoa, what was that?

Excuse You!

Pee-yew! Your red blood cell just passed gas . . . well, actually it released the oxygen it was carrying—and this type of gas doesn't really smell. The oxygen passed through the capillary wall (good thing these walls are so thin!) and was picked up by a body cell. Then the body cell released carbon dioxide (CO_2, a waste product), which passed through the capillary wall and was picked up by red blood cells.

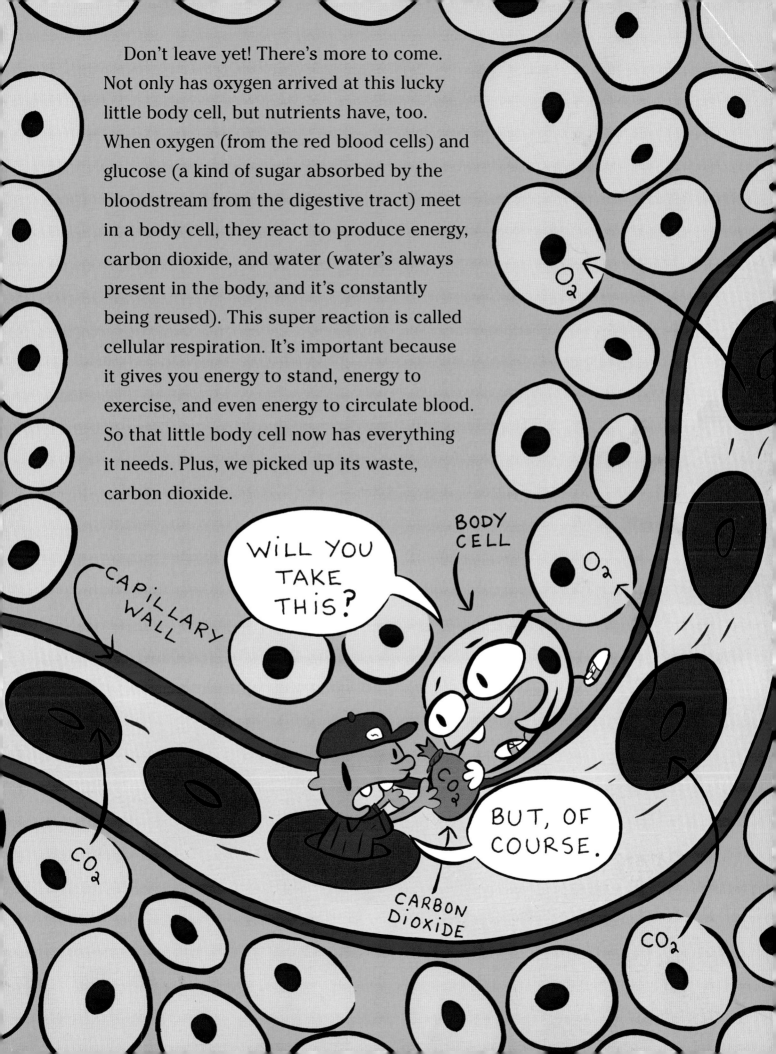

Don't leave yet! There's more to come. Not only has oxygen arrived at this lucky little body cell, but nutrients have, too. When oxygen (from the red blood cells) and glucose (a kind of sugar absorbed by the bloodstream from the digestive tract) meet in a body cell, they react to produce energy, carbon dioxide, and water (water's always present in the body, and it's constantly being reused). This super reaction is called cellular respiration. It's important because it gives you energy to stand, energy to exercise, and even energy to circulate blood. So that little body cell now has everything it needs. Plus, we picked up its waste, carbon dioxide.

Nowhere to Go but Up

The red blood cell you're on and the others around you have done their job—they've carried oxygen to the body cells. Now it's time to travel into a vein and head back toward the heart. Veins are blood vessels that are thinner than arteries but thicker than capillaries. But . . . thud . . . what did you just bump into?

It was a valve. You'd better watch which way you're going! Like the heart, many veins have a cool way of preventing blood from flowing back the wrong way—one-way venous valves. These valves not only keep blood from going backward, they also help blood "climb" up to the heart as it travels against gravity.

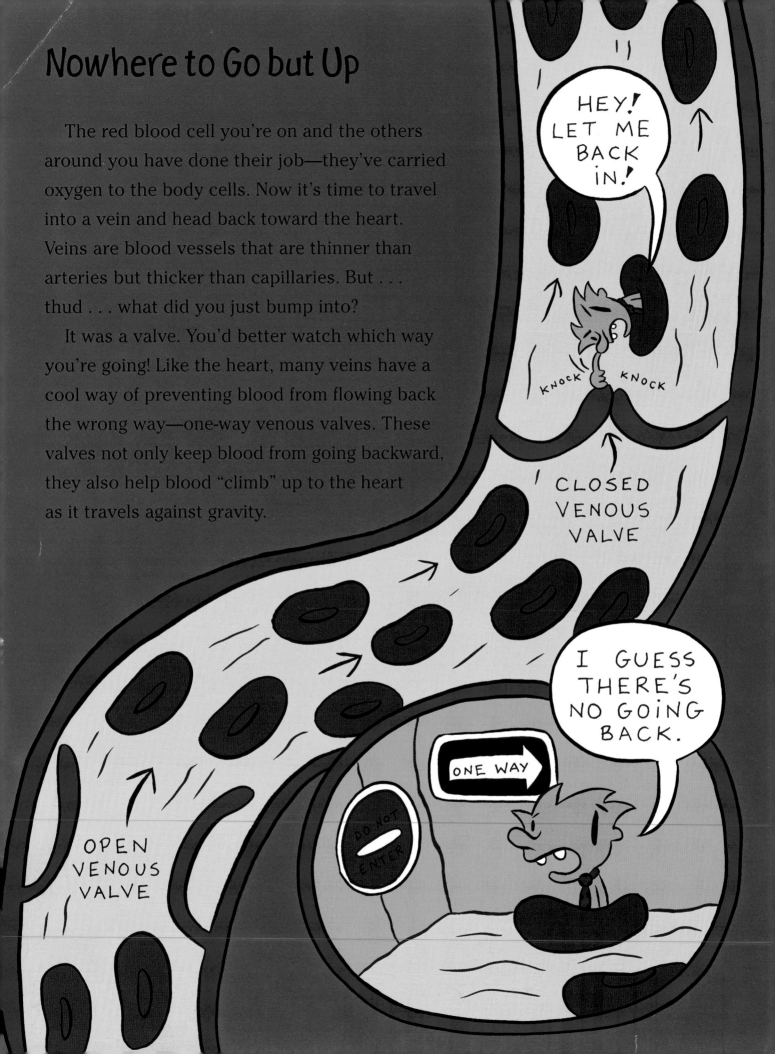

Human, We Have a Problem

Here you are in the right leg, ready to return to the heart, but look out! There's an army of leukocytes (a.k.a. white blood cells) headed your way. What on earth is going on?

The white blood cells are responding to a cut on the leg. Better stand back. These white blood cells are going to engulf the invading bacteria that have made their way into the body through the skin. The rod-shaped bacteria could cause an infection in the body.

Go, Army!

White blood cells are one of the three components of blood. Like red blood cells, they usually travel through the bloodstream. Unlike red blood cells, troops of white blood cells can move through tissue into parts of the body. Don't look for these cells to be dressed in camouflage, though—not all these soldiers look alike. Some, like macrophages and B cells, look different from each other and do different jobs.

Like an army, macrophages increase in number, surround the invaders, and destroy the bad guys. Keep up the good work, Mac!

B lymphocytes, or B cells, are another kind of white blood cell. They make antibodies—chemicals that help protect you against certain diseases. Antibodies also give you immunity from that disease, meaning they help prevent you from getting it again.

ATTACK!

That's Pus, Gus

If not cared for properly, some cuts may get infected. A yellowish fluid called pus can indicate infection. A cut with pus needs proper medical help.

To help prevent infections, wash the cut with soap and water, then cover it with a bandage.

Clot a Lot

What a battle! As all this action is happening, more troops—
platelets, the last of the three components of blood—arrive
on the scene. These little guys, with the help of special fibers
called fibrin, help to form a clot that stops the blood from
flowing out of the wound. Soon the clot becomes a scab,
which gives the damaged skin time to heal. Don't pick at it!

Inferior or Superior?

You've come a long way from that little cell that passed gas. In fact, you're in a vein called the inferior vena cava, and you're almost back to the heart. You have completed a trip through one part, or circuit, of the body's circulatory system— the systemic circuit. This circuit nourishes most of the body with blood.

Now there's nothing inferior about the inferior vena cava: it just means that blood going through it has been in the lower part of the body. If you had been in the upper body, you would have gone through the superior vena cava. The blood in both of these veins is oxygen-poor, or deoxygenated, because a lot of the oxygen from the red blood cells was given to the body cells.

RIGHT ATRIUM OF HEART

ALMOST THERE!

Systemic Circulation

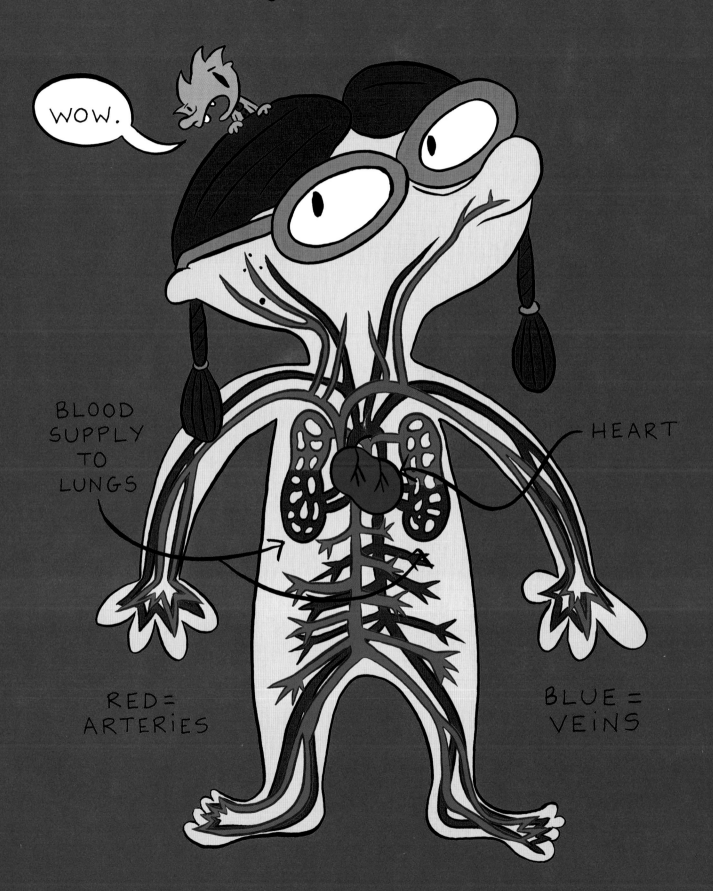

Déjà Vu?

The inferior vena cava brings you into the heart at the right atrium. Then it's down through the tricuspid valve, which works just like the mitral valve but is located between the right atrium and the right ventricle. It feels like we've done something like this before. . . .

How Shocking!

Before you leave for the right ventricle, there's something in the right atrium that you might like to check out—the sinoatrial node. This most amazing little group of cells is known as the heart's natural pacemaker. It sends electrical signals to the atria and ventricles, telling them to beat at a certain pace, or rate. So when a person is exercising, the heart's chambers will contract more quickly, sending more blood, and therefore more oxygen, to the body cells than when a person is at rest and doesn't need as much oxygen. Did you get a charge out of that?

SINO-ATRIAL NODE

I ... SING ... THE BODY ... ELECTRIC ...

THUMP

Time to Fill 'Er Up

The next part of the circulatory system, the pulmonary circuit, is shorter but no less important. Pulmonary refers to lungs, and that's where you're headed.

After saying good-bye to the right ventricle, say hello to the pulmonary valve and the pulmonary artery. This is the artery that will bring you into the lungs. Take a deep breath—you're here for oxygen.

CO_2

O_2

CO_2

CO_2

PULMONARY ARTERY

MAGNIFIED A BUNCH OF TIMES

TRACHEA

BRONCHUS

PULMONARY VEINS

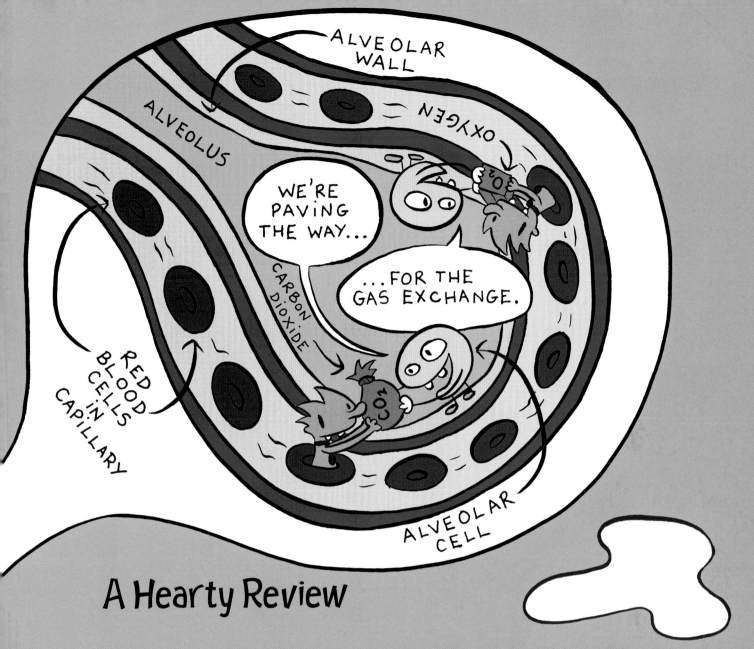

A Hearty Review

Have you ever traded part of your lunch for a part of your friend's lunch? Well, it's the same in your lungs: carbon dioxide is breathed out when you exhale, and oxygen is taken into the body from the air when you inhale. Sounds like a good trade.

Now, do you remember when the red blood cells released oxygen to the body cells? They got that oxygen here in the lungs. Do you also remember that the body cells passed their carbon dioxide to the red blood cells? Now it's time for the red blood cells to get rid of that waste gas at the lungs.

This gas exchange takes place in the lungs' alveoli, or air sacs. Capillaries surround the alveoli. As you saw earlier, capillaries are so thin that the gases are easily exchanged here. Isn't that refreshing?

Heartward Bound

After this great gas exchange, the blood goes back to the heart. This blood is called oxygenated blood because of all the oxygen it's carrying. Can you guess which side the blood goes into?

Yes, it goes to the heart's left side, and blood will now be pumped out of the left ventricle and on to the body's cells.

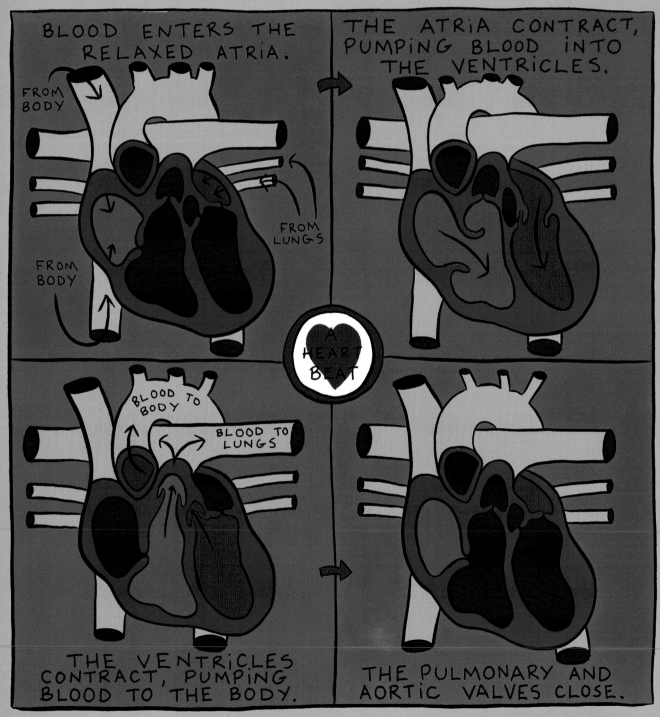

BLOOD ENTERS THE RELAXED ATRIA.

FROM BODY

FROM LUNGS

FROM BODY

THE ATRIA CONTRACT, PUMPING BLOOD INTO THE VENTRICLES.

A HEART BEAT

THE VENTRICLES CONTRACT, PUMPING BLOOD TO THE BODY.

BLOOD TO BODY

BLOOD TO LUNGS

THE PULMONARY AND AORTIC VALVES CLOSE.

Heart-to-Heart

The last part of the circulatory system is the coronary circuit. It's the shortest circuit in the body, but it's important because it supplies the heart itself with blood. As blood leaves the left ventricle through the aorta, blood vessels called coronary arteries branch off the base of the aorta and bring blood to the heart cells. Without this supply, the heart cells couldn't survive. Coronary veins carry blood away from the heart.

Fighting Plaque

Oh, no . . . look at that sticky gunk on the walls of this coronary artery. It's plaque—no, not the kind that can build up on your teeth. The plaque in arteries is a fatty substance. An unhealthy diet, especially lots of fatty foods, can cause plaque to build up in people's arteries, which can lead to a clog in a coronary artery. Think of the pipes below your kitchen sink. If too much gunk builds up, water can't pass through the pipes. Then it's time to get the plunger.

Adults with lots of plaque in their coronary arteries are at risk of having a heart attack. Some of this nasty plaque may prevent blood from reaching heart cells. Without oxygen, these cells become damaged. When this happens, a doctor has to unclog that artery.

Treating your heart well helps prevent heart trouble. Two heart-smart ideas are to eat right and to exercise. This way the heart can be buff and healthy. This advice is straight from the heart!

The Circulatory Story

You've visited three kinds of blood vessels, hungry body cells, and the four chambers of the heart; plus you've seen breathtaking views of the lungs. If you'd like to go again, you'll have plenty of chances to catch a ride, because the heart beats about one hundred thousand times per day. Blood circulates through the body over and over and over, each day of your life. Many things must happen in just the right order to ensure that everything in this incredible body system works properly.

So the next time you feel your heart beating or think about your veins or get a scrape, remember your trip through the circulatory story. You must admit, it sure is great to circulate!

AROUND AND AROUND...

THOUSANDS OF TIMES EACH DAY...

SPIN

SPIN

Glossary

alveolus (plural: alveoli): A small air sac in the lungs where the gas exchange (carbon dioxide for oxygen) occurs.

antibody: A chemical made by the body's immune system to help prevent or fight some diseases.

aorta: The body's largest artery through which blood travels from the left ventricle of the heart to the rest of the body, with the exception of the lungs.

aortic valve: A heart valve located between the left ventricle and the aorta.

artery: A blood vessel that carries blood away from the heart.

atrium (plural: atria): One of the top two chambers, or rooms, of the heart that receives blood from veins.

B lymphocyte (B cell): A type of white blood cell that makes antibodies, which destroy invaders.

bacterium (plural: bacteria): A tiny, one-celled organism. There are many species of bacteria; some are helpful to humans, others are harmful.

blood pressure: The measurement of pressure that blood puts on the walls of blood vessels, especially arteries.

blood vessel: A tube in which blood travels throughout the body.

capillary: A tiny, one-cell-thick blood vessel that carries blood between an artery and a vein.

carbon dioxide: A waste gas released by body cells and exhaled from the body via the lungs; CO_2.

cellular respiration: The reaction that occurs when glucose and oxygen, in the presence of water, meet in body cells; the result is the release of carbon dioxide and energy.

circulatory system: A body system made up of the heart, blood vessels, and blood. It circulates, or delivers, blood, oxygen, nutrients, water, and some hormones throughout the body.

clot: A thick substance formed by fibers and platelets in the blood as a result of a cut in the skin.

coronary artery: One of two arteries through which blood travels to nourish the cells of the heart.

coronary circuit: One of three parts of the body's circulatory system. This circuit supplies blood to heart cells.

deoxygenated blood: Blood that contains a reduced amount of oxygen; deoxygenated blood travels through most veins and through the right side of the heart.

erythrocyte (red blood cell): One of three cellular components of blood; red blood cells deliver oxygen, which is picked up in the lungs, to body cells.

fibrin: A protein that helps clot blood.

glucose: A type of sugar absorbed by the bloodstream from the digestive tract and used by the body for cellular respiration.

heart attack: An event that can cause chest pains, fainting, or in worst cases, death; a heart attack can be due to a blockage in a blood vessel that leads to the heart.

hemoglobin: A protein found in red blood cells that transports, or carries, oxygen.

immunity: A state of being able to prevent getting a disease.

infection: Sickness brought on by bacteria, viruses, or fungi.

inferior vena cava: A vein that carries blood from the lower part of the body to the heart's right atrium.

leukocyte (white blood cell): One of three cellular components of blood; white blood cells help defend and protect the body against invaders.

lung: One of two organs located in the chest in which carbon dioxide is exchanged for oxygen.

macrophage: A white blood cell that surrounds and engulfs invaders.

mitral valve: A heart valve located between the left atrium and the left ventricle.

oxygen: A chemical element found in air and inhaled into the lungs; O_2.

oxygenated blood: Oxygen-rich blood; oxygenated blood travels through most arteries and through the left side of the heart.

pericardium: A protective sac that encloses the heart.

plaque: A fatty substance that can build up in blood vessels and cause a clog.

plasma: The liquid part of blood; 90% of plasma is water.

platelet: One of three cellular components of blood; platelets help blood to clot.

pulmonary: Referring to the lungs.

pulmonary artery: A blood vessel that carries blood from the right ventricle of the heart to the lungs.

pulmonary circuit: One of three parts of the body's circulatory system. This circuit carries blood to the lungs and back to the heart.

pulmonary valve: A heart valve located between the right ventricle and the pulmonary artery.

pulmonary vein: A blood vessel that carries blood from the lungs to the left atrium.

pus: A yellowish substance that can form after a foreign object enters the body; pus may indicate infection.

scab: A natural covering that is formed by the body after a cut; a scab gives a wound time to heal.

septum: The membrane that separates the left and the right sides of the heart.

sinoatrial node: The heart's natural pacemaker, which sends electrical signals to the heart's chambers so they contract at the correct rate.

superior vena cava: The vein in which blood travels from the upper body, including the head, to the heart's right atrium.

systemic circuit: One of three parts of the body's circulatory system. This circuit carries blood throughout the body and returns it to the heart.

tricuspid valve: A heart valve located between the right atrium and the right ventricle.

valve: One-way "doors" that keep blood traveling in the right direction.

vein: A blood vessel that carries blood toward the heart.

ventricle: One of two bottom chambers of the heart that receives blood from the atrium and sends it out of the heart through an artery.

Websites

Heart Anatomy Glossary Printout—
EnchantedLearning.com
http://www.enchantedlearning.com/subjects/
anatomy/heart/labelinterior/glossary.shtml
Offers a glossary of important terms and
information about the heart. Readers can
print out a heart diagram.

Kids Health
http://kidshealth.org/kid/
This site's "How the Body Works" section
has specific information on parts of the
body, including the heart.

Let's Learn About Your Heart!
http://www.mplsheartfoundation.org/kids/
Minneapolis Heart Institute Foundation's
site teaches children heart basics and
shows healthy choices they can make to
keep their hearts healthy.

Further Reading

Calabresi, Linda. *Human Body*. New York:
Simon & Schuster Books for Young
Readers, 2008.

Seymour, Simon. *The Heart: Our Circulatory
System*. New York: HarperCollins, 2006.

Walker, Richard. *Encyclopedia of the Human
Body*. New York: DK Publishing, 2002.

Bibliography

Phibbs, Brendan. *The Human Heart: A Basic
Guide to Heart Disease*. Philadelphia:
Lippincott Williams & Wilkins, 2007.

Gray, Henry. *Anatomy of the Human Body*,
30th edition. Philadelphia: Lea & Febiger,
1985.

Marieb, Elaine N. *Anatomy & Physiology*. San
Francisco: Benjamin Cummings, 2002.